Australia

Come on a journey of discovery

Linda Pickwell

QED Publishing

QED

First published in the UK in 2004 by
QED Publishing
A division of Quarto Publishing plc
The Fitzpatrick Building
188–194 York Way, London N7 9QP

A Catalogue record for this book is available from
the British Library.

ISBN 1 84538 058 4

Written by Linda Pickwell
Designed by Starry Dog Books Ltd
Editor Christine Harvey
Map by PCGraphics (UK) Ltd

Creative Director Louise Morley
Editorial Manager Jean Coppendale

Printed and bound in China

The words in **bold**
are explained in the
Glossary on page 28.

Contents

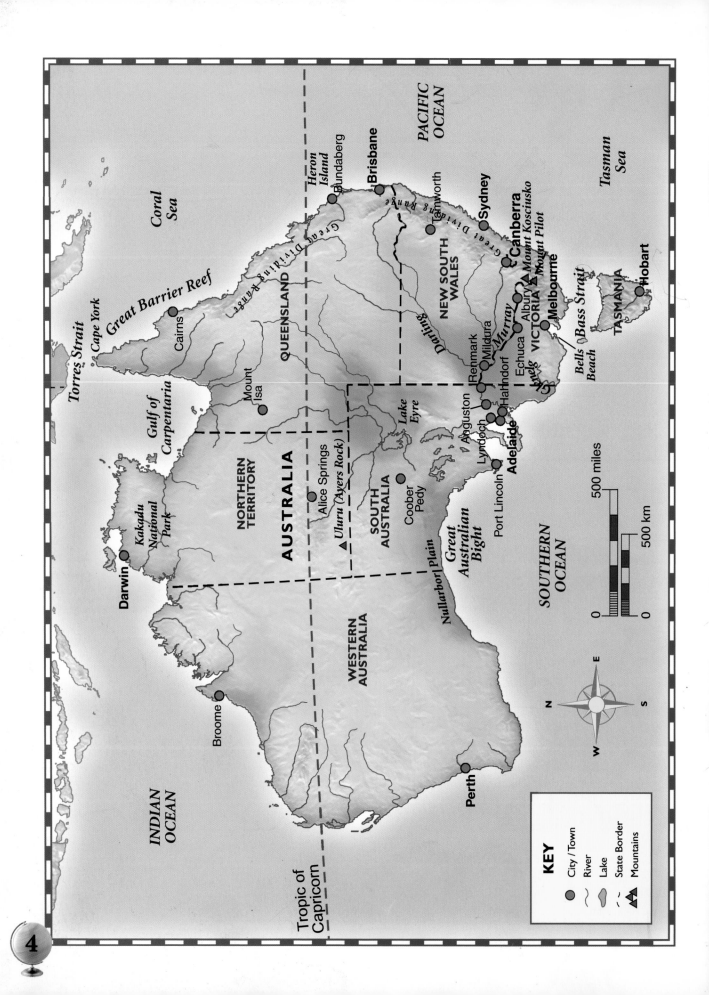

PACIFIC OCEAN

Tasman Sea

Coral Sea

Heron Island
Bundaberg
Brisbane
Tamworth
Sydney
Canberra
Mount Kosciusko
Mount Pilot
Albury
Murray
Melbourne
Mildura
Renmark
Echuca
Hahndorf
Glenelg
VICTORIA
Bells Beach
Bass Strait
TASMANIA
Hobart
NEW SOUTH WALES
Darling
Great Dividing Range

Torres Strait
Cape York
Great Barrier Reef
Cairns
QUEENSLAND
Great Dividing Range

Gulf of Carpentaria

Mount Isa

NORTHERN TERRITORY

AUSTRALIA

Alice Springs
Uluru (Ayers Rock)

Lake Eyre

SOUTH AUSTRALIA

Coober Pedy

Angaston
Lyndoch
Adelaide
Port Lincoln

Great Australian Bight

Nullarbor Plain

SOUTHERN OCEAN

Kakadu National Park

Darwin

WESTERN AUSTRALIA

Broome

Perth

INDIAN OCEAN

Tropic of Capricorn

500 miles

500 km

N
E
S
W

KEY
City / Town
River
Lake
State Border
Mountains

4

Where in the world is Australia?

Australia lies south of the Asian **continent**. It is the smallest continent in the world, but one of the largest countries. About 18 million people live in Australia, most of them in towns and cities near the coast.

Did you know?

The island of Tasmania is part of Australia. It lies 300km off the south-eastern coast, near Melbourne. Long ago, it was linked to the mainland of Australia, but was separated after the last Ice age when the Bass Strait was formed by rising water levels.

▼ Australia and its place in the world.

Australia

▲ The national flag of Australia.

Did you know?

Name
Commonwealth of Australia
Location
South of the continent of Asia
Nearest neighbours
Papua New Guinea, Indonesia and Malaysia to the north, New Zealand to the south east
Surrounding oceans
Pacific Ocean, Indian Ocean, Southern Ocean
Length of coastline 25 760km
Capital Canberra in ACT (Australian Capital Territory)
Area 7 772 535km^2
Population 18 000 000
Life expectancy Male 75, Female 80
Religion Christian
Languages Australian English and many Aboriginal languages
Climate Generally arid, temperate in the south and east, **tropical** in the north
Highest mountain range
Mount Kosciusko (2228m)
Major rivers Murray (length: 1930km), Darling (length: 1879km)
Currency Australian dollar

What is Australia like?

The regions

Australia is the flattest and driest **continent** on Earth. It is nicknamed 'the land down under' and it is a huge, hot and spectacular country that in many places can seem completely deserted. This is not surprising, as ninety per cent of the population live in the cities and towns around the coast.

Australia is also home to some of the strangest wildlife on the planet, as well as the most lovable. It is also a country of great natural beauty.

▼ Kimberley in north west Australia is one of the world's last great areas of wilderness.

Australia is made up of states and territories that were developed and named when explorers arrived and began to settle. The mainland has six major regions – New South Wales, Victoria, Queensland, South Australia, Western Australia and Northern Territory.

The outback

Three-quarters of the country is made up of vast, almost empty areas of desert or semi-desert known as the 'outback'. There are few people here, and little vegetation. The people who do live here mainly work on sheep and cattle farms , called 'stations'.

Western Australia

The vast **plateau** in the inland part of Western Australia is rich in ancient rocks and minerals. Since the area was discovered, miners have endured heat and discomfort there in the hope of striking gold. Australia is the world's largest producer of industrial diamonds and opals.

The Great Dividing Range

This series of mountain ranges stretches from Cape York at the northern tip of Queensland to the Bass Strait in the south.

The Central Basin

This flat area stretches from the Gulf of Carpentaria in the north, to the mouth of the Murray River in the south. Once it was an inland sea.

▲ 'The Three Sisters' rock formations are at Katoomba, in the Blue Mountains near Sydney. At night they are floodlit.

Australia has a number of national parks. Jon visited one called Kakadu and wrote to his English pen-pal about it.

I visited the Kakadu National Park yesterday, where **Crocodile Dundee** was filmed. I saw the cave paintings done by the Aboriginal people, and went on a dawn cruise along the Yellow Water to see the birds and the crocodiles. It was awesome!

◄ Australian crocodiles can run fast on land and can leap up out of the water to catch and drown their prey

Climate

Around the country

Australia has a **tropical** or near-tropical climate. Two thirds of the land is desert or shrub land, and has little rainfall. These areas can be hot during the day, but cold at night. The **interior** has little rainfall, and long droughts occur. Rainfall is important, as it is needed to sustain all plant and animal life.

The seasons

The summer months in Australia are December to February and they are hot throughout the country. If you travelled here on Christmas Day you might spend it on the beach! The winter months, June to August, are usually the coolest and wettest.

The north

People who live in the north say that there are only two seasons there – the dry and the wet. During the wet months of October to March, there can be **monsoon** rains and even cyclones. Humidity is also very high and mosquitoes are a pest.

The south

The southern areas have warm summers and mild winters.

The east

Winds blowing from the Pacific Ocean and rising over the Great Dividing Range can bring heavy rains in late spring, summer and early autumn.

▼ A few tough native plants manage to survive in the semi-desert areas.

Maximum temperatures

City	January	April	July	October
Darwin	32°C	33°C	31°C	34°C
Perth	29°C	24°C	17°C	21°C
Melbourne	26°C	20°C	13°C	19°C
Brisbane	29°C	26°C	20°C	27°C

Average monthly rainfall

City	January	April	July	October
Darwin	386mm	97mm	0mm	51mm
Perth	8mm	43mm	170mm	56mm
Melbourne	48mm	58mm	48mm	66mm
Brisbane	163mm	94mm	56mm	64mm

▼ Surfer's Paradise, south of Brisbane, is a very popular beach. In the hot sun, people are advised to protect their skin and wear a t-shirt and a hat.

Australia's wildlife

Unique plants and animals

One of Australia's main attractions is its incredible range of plants and curious animals. For example, the duck-billed platypus that looks like a fantasy creature made up for a children's story book. There are more than 25 000 species of plants and around 250 000 species of animal life in Australia.

The **tropical** rainforests in the east are some of the oldest **eco-systems** in the world. The tree kangaroo and the bird wing butterfly live in this **habitat**.

The Australian bush

Near the coast, in the east, south east and south west, are open woodlands. These areas are generally referred to as the Australian bush. Eucalyptus trees grow here and they are so hardy they can survive drought, bushfires and poor soil. Grey kangaroos and koalas live only in these areas.

Australia is famous for **marsupials**. These are extinct everywhere else in the world, except for South America. The best known are the koala, wallaby, kangaroo, possum and the wombat. Birds such as kookaburras, parrots and budgerigars are also found in the bush.

Dangerous creatures

You will find more highly dangerous spiders and reptiles in Australia than anywhere else in the world. The most fearsome spider is the redback and the deadliest snake is the taipan. The most dangerous animal to humans is the salt-water crocodile of northern Australia.

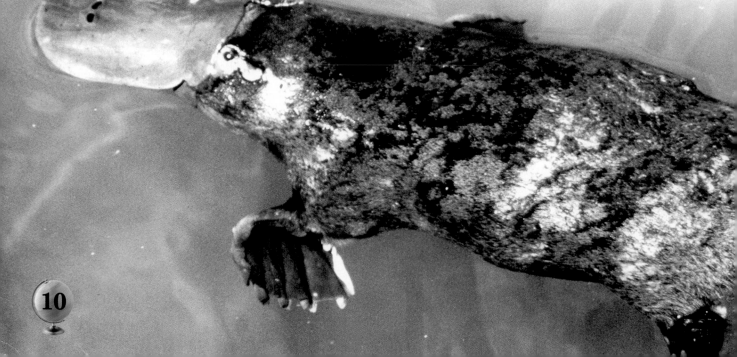

Jenny went to the Cleland Wildlife Park on Mount Lofty, near to Adelaide where she lives. She wrote about it in her diary.

The park was an area of bush. We were able to walk among the animals. I saw kangaroos and wallabies, and an emu – a big bird that can't fly. There was also an aviary where we could see the birds up close. But the best part was taking photographs of the sleepy koalas.

▲ Grey kangaroos can hop at a top speed of 60 kilometres an hour!

▼ The web-footed platypus is the size of a small pet cat, with a bill like a duck's and a tail like a beaver's.

◀ Australia has many colourful birds, including budgerigars, parrots, finches and cockatoos.

Travelling around Australia

By air

Australia has a number of international airports, in Sydney, Melbourne, Perth, Brisbane, Cairns, Adelaide, Darwin and Hobart in Tasmania. In 1934, the airline QANTAS began some of the first international flights in the world.

Because the country is so huge, and trains can be slow, 80 per cent of people make long distance trips inside Australia by air. There are plenty of smaller airports, which is very convenient if you are visiting for only a short time.

▶ John Flynn started the Flying Doctor service in 1928.

▼ In 1885 Melbourne's first tram made the journey from the city to the suburbs. Trams are just as popular today.

The Flying Doctor

For many people living in the **interior** the nearest hospital may be several hours away by car. To help overcome this problem, the Flying Doctor service was started. Doctors use small, lightweight planes to reach remote **settlements** or homesteads.

By train

Australia's rail network does not reach all areas of the country. Most main lines are around the coast. There is one major line across the centre of the country, from the main cities in the south to Darwin. Sleeping overnight on a train can be an adventure, and

Journey	Distance	Flying time
Sydney to Perth	3400km	5 hours
Adelaide to Darwin	2600km	3½ hours

many people make special train journeys to see the country. The trains offering this service are like hotels on wheels. One of the best known is the Indian Pacific train, which takes three days to travel from Sydney to Perth. The train crosses the Nullarbor **Plain**, a vast part of the Great Victoria Desert in Western Australia, on the world's longest length of straight track.

By road

Today, there is a national highway network, linking all the capital cities of the regions. Most goods are transported by road. Road transporters can be three to five 'trucks' long. Most Australians own a car and use the highway systems. In cities there is a mix of car, bus and tram travel, and Sydney has an overhead monorail service.

Travelling through the cities

◀ Canberra is the home of Australia's High Court and the National University. It is also the financial heart of Australia and the centre of government.

▼ Adelaide hosts many popular arts festivals.

Canberra

This is the capital city of Australia in the state of New South Wales. It was originally a small sheep station by the Molonglo River. Travelling here today you will see that it is the country's political centre. It is a modern city with shops and restaurants, as well as having nearby areas of national parklands.

Adelaide

In 1836, the flat **plain** between the Mount Lofty Ranges was chosen as the place to build the city of Adelaide, the capital of South Australia. Travelling here you will see many 19th-century public buildings, including the state library, museum and art gallery. Although proud of its past, the city is very modern, with many shops and theatres.

▲ There is lots to do in Perth, including surfing, fishing, yacht racing and humpback whale-watching.

Perth

Perth, on the west coast, is Australia's most isolated state capital. It lies on the Swan River, 10km from the Indian Ocean. From the first settlers' houses, the city has grown as the gold rush and mining brought wealth to the area. On one side of the city are long stretches of beach, and inland, many parks.

Melbourne

Melbourne, on the south coast, is a relaxed city with a wide range of sports and outdoor activities. The city is a mix of impressive skyscrapers and 19th-century buildings; you can even travel around by old-fashioned tram. Nearby are areas of great natural beauty, such as Philip Island, the Yarra Valley and the Dandenong mountain foothills.

Brisbane

On the east coast, Brisbane is surrounded by green and hilly suburbs. The centre is a mix of modern buildings made of glass and steel, and 19th-century buildings. Within the city is a bustling area with an Asian community, known as China Town.

A tour of Sydney

Emma and Andrew are twins. They live in Sydney in New South Wales. Their English cousins are coming to visit and the twins have made a guide of what to see and do in the city.

Circular Quay

Sydney is a big city and can be split into four areas. Our favourite is Circular Quay. It is the oldest part, dating back to 1788 when the first prison ships arrived from Britain. We sometimes go to the Sydney Opera House, which has theatres and concert halls. It is on Bennelong Point, which sticks out into the harbour.

Royal Botanic Gardens

We like the quiet part of the city best. There is a large park in Sydney called the Royal Botanic Gardens. It was created in 1816 and has two glasshouses that hold mini tropical **ecosystems**. We will take you to the Governor's private garden, which is now open to the public. Open-air concerts are held here. We can take a picnic!

Did you know?

Sydney Opera House facts:

It holds 3000 events per year.

It has an annual audience of two million people.

It has over one million roof tiles.

Darling Harbour

We'll also have to take you to Darling Harbour. There's so much to do there. You can visit the huge aquarium and walk along a clear underwater tunnel with colourful fish swimming all around you. It feels as if you're walking on the sea floor! There's also a gigantic movie screen – the biggest we've ever seen, and a real Chinese garden with great big fish in the pond.

Sydney Harbour Bridge

Another famous sight is the Sydney Harbour Bridge, finished in 1932. Visitors can now walk over the top of the bridge. The view's fantastic from there. Sydney is an important business and shopping centre. It is always busy during the day with workers and shoppers, and at night with people going to restaurants and theatres.

The Great Barrier Reef

History of the Great Barrier Reef

This is a natural wonder found off the Queensland coast. It is the largest **coral** reef in the world. Coral can be dated back at least 500 million years.

The Great Barrier Reef began about 18 000 years ago during the last Ice age. It is a major tourist attraction and is protected by the Marine Park Authority established by an Act of Parliament in 1975. People from all over the world travel to the area to experience diving, snorkelling or to look at the colourful coral reef from glass-bottomed boats.

More than 2000 species of fish and countless numbers of corals, both hard and soft, are found in these waters.

▼ The coral reef is a fragile ecosystem.

▼ Shoals of reef fish are every colour of the rainbow.

When Scott stayed with his friend Tom in Cairns Tom's dad took them to the Great Barrier Reef. Scott wrote to his family about the amazing sights he saw there.

I wish you could be here. We had a trip in a glass-bottomed boat. We could look down at the fish and coral – it was amazing! We saw a great shoal of bat fish, which live in colonies. There were lots of colourful, small fish and a moray eel, which must have been 2 metres long. Even better have been the two times we were able to snorkel. Being in the water and so close to the wildlife is brilliant. Yesterday, potato cod were swimming alongside us and a manta ray came close enough to touch.

Mum, Dad & Chloe
34 Wongaboo Rise
Mellhill
Vangswith
2905WA

▼ Divers should be careful not to touch the coral or it will be damaged.

Travelling along the Murray River

The source of the river

The Murray River is the largest river in Australia and provides essential water. The **source** of the river is near Mount Kosciusko in the Snowy Mountains, part of the eastern mountain ranges. The river has been known to dry up on at least three occasions. The river flows through the city of Adelaide and into the Great Australian Bight.

The upper river

The upper river cuts through the eastern mountains. It flows west and north west, forming most of the New South Wales and Victoria **state** boundaries. The central section lies on a floodplain with a number of **tributaries** joining it.

▼ A paddle steamer on the Murray River.

QUEENSLAND

SOUTH AUSTRALIA

Lake Eyre

Warrego

Culgoa

Barwon

Great Dividing Range

NEW SOUTH WALES

Darling

Lachlan

Murray

Renmark

Mildura

Murrumbidgee

Adelaide

Murray

Albury

Echuca

Barmah Forest

Mount Kosciusko

SOUTHERN OCEAN

VICTORIA

Mount Pilot

Tasman Sea

EMMYLOU

Monitoring the water

The importance of the Murray River for drinking water and **irrigation** led to the formation of the River Valley Commission in 1915. It is responsible for developing **hydro-electric power** and monitoring the quality and use of the water.

The history of the river

Paddle steamers were important in developing **settlements** along the Murray River. They were used to carry goods between areas. An ex-convict, Henry Hopwood, began a ferry crossing service at Echuca in 1835.

Echuca eventually became the largest inland port in Australia.

Today, the town has developed this history of the river into a tourist attraction. There are horse-drawn carriages on the streets and paddle steamers on the river, so that people can see what the river and the areas around it used to be like.

Drew is doing a project on the history of the Murray River at school.

Water from the Murray River was first used for irrigation in 1887 when the Canadian brothers William and George Chaffey came to the town of Mildura. They established an irrigation system there. Mildura has now grown into a modern city surrounded by a region growing vines, olives and citrus fruits.

The Barossa Valley

▲ At many of the wineries you can watch the wine being made.

The Barossa Valley is the major wine-producing area of South Australia. It lies 48km north east of the city of Adelaide in the Mount Lofty Ranges.

The history of the Barossa Valley

The area was first settled in 1842 by German immigrants who established the villages of Tanunda, Lyndoch and Light's Pass. The climate helped them to farm the land. The winter rains and warm summers encouraged good crops to grow in the soil. Grapes soon became the major crop and many wineries developed.

Tourist attractions

Travelling to this area, it is easy to see that the early German influence is still obvious in the style of the buildings and place names, and the region's food, music and festivals.

Some of the largest wineries are now open to the public as tourist attractions. The Collingrove Homestead at Anguston is now owned by the National Trust. It was built in 1856 and has been preserved to show the original furnishings.

▼ A view of the vines being grown in the Barossa Valley.

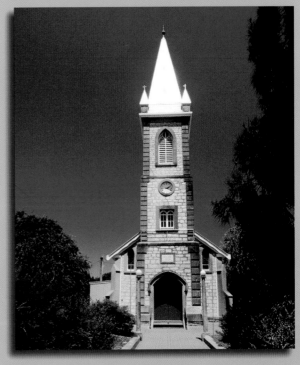

▲ This Lutheran church is in Hahndorf, named after Dirk Hahn, the captain of the first settlers' ship.

As a birthday treat, Anna asked for a trip to Hahndorf. She wrote about her day there in her diary.

My great-great-grandfather lived in Germany as a small child before he moved to South Australia. The first settlers arrived in Hahndorf from Germany in 1838 on a ship called the 'Zebra'. I liked looking at the German-style houses. There were many things on sale in the shops, like special German foods, gifts and sweets. I had a ride through the town on a horse-drawn carriage. I enjoyed the atmosphere and tried to imagine what life would have been like for the settlers.

23

Alice Springs and Uluru

Alice Springs

Alice Springs is the main **settlement** in the 'Red Centre', a large area of desert and rocky ridges in the Northern Territory. It became a staging post in 1871 for the overland telegraph line and is named after Alice Todd, the wife of the line's construction manager.

There was no proper surfaced road until the 1940s. Today, the railway and the cross-continental **Stuart Highway** make it an important transport town for beef and minerals.

Tourist attraction

Alice Springs is a major tourist attraction, with an average of 400 000 visitors every year. Travelling there, you will see the Museum of Central Australia, original settlement buildings and the only winery in central Australia, Chateau Hornsby.

Uluru

Many visitors to Alice Springs visit the Uluru-Kata Tjuta National Park, which contains one of Australia's most famous landmarks, Uluru (the Aboriginal name for Ayers Rock). This giant rock is made of a type of sandstone called arkosic, which seems to change colour according to the light. It is often photographed at sunset when it looks a fiery red-orange colour.

Uluru is oval shaped, 3.6km in length and 2km wide. Shallow caves that are sacred to the **Aborigines** lie at the base of the rock. They contain carvings and paintings. Some of the more sacred sites are fenced off.

The Aborigines

Uluru is an important place in the culture of the Anangu Aborigines. In 1985 ownership of this site was formally handed back to them.

▼ Uluru stands 335m above the surrounding flat desert.

▲ In 2004 the city of Darwin was added to the Ghan train's route from Adelaide.

▶ This Aboriginal rock art of handprints may be 4000 years old.

The Aborigines

The history of the Aborigines

The **Aborigines** are the original inhabitants of Australia, and can be traced back 40 000 years. When Europeans came to claim Australia, many Aborigines were killed in fights over land. During the 1850s Aborigines were placed in **reserves**.

Aboriginal people now form 1.6 per cent of the population in Australia. Only recently has there been a real acceptance of their rights and some land given back to them.

Boomerangs

Traditionally, Aborigines lived as nomadic hunters. They used special sticks called boomerangs. The boomerang was used in a variety of ways – as a weapon, in traditional

games and even for poking a fire! Over time the shape has changed and now the stick curves and returns to the thrower when hurled. Many boomerangs are decorated with pictures telling stories and myths.

Dreamtime

The Aborigines base much of their culture on 'Dreamtime'. These are special stories that started as myths about the creation of the world. The Aborigines believe that giant creatures called 'creation ancestors' created the world with their movements.

Aborigine children

Most Aborigine children attend state schools. The Australian government now insists on equal opportunities for all and have included Aboriginal culture in the school curriculum.

▲ Young Aborigine children surf the Internet for study and for fun.

▲ Boomerang means 'throwing stick'.

Namatjira goes to a small school in the outback. This is an extract from his diary.

◄ Aboriginal art, painted on bark or canvas, is in great demand from art galleries, particularly Australian ones.

Today we performed a special dance for some visitors to our school. It was a sequence about a serpent creating flat lands with its sideways movements. We told them what Dreamtime is and how we had represented the movements and moods of nature in our dance. I hope they enjoyed it.

Glossary

Aborigine
the original inhabitants of Australia

adapted
Changed to suit the environment

continent
one of the seven large areas of land on the Earth's surface: Africa, Asia, Australasia, Antarctica, North America, South America, Europe.

coral
hard material that forms from the skeletons of tiny sea animals

ecosystem
living creatures and their environment, and how they affect each other

hydro-electric power
electricity made from the controlled flow of water

interior
central land not near to the coast

irrigation
supplying water to the land, usually to support agriculture

marsupials
mammals that carry their young in a pouch

monsoon
the rainy season – heavy downpours often experienced in hot countries

plain
an extensive area of low level land

plateau
an extensive area of high, mainly level land

reserve
public land set aside for housing certain groups of people

settlement
a place where people set up a community

source
where a river or stream starts

Stuart Highway
a major highway crossing the country and passing through Alice Springs. Named after the explorer John McDougall Stuart

tributaries
rivers or streams that runs into another, often larger, one

tropical
a climate that is hat, wet and humid

Index

Teaching ideas and activities for children

The following activities address and develop the geographical 'enquiry' approach, and promote thinking skills and creativity. The activities in section A have been devised to help children develop higher order thinking, based on Bloom's taxonomy of thinking. The activities in section B have been devised to promote different types of learning styles, based on Howard Gardner's theory of multiple intelligences.

A: ACTIVITIES TO DEVELOP THINKING SKILLS

ACTIVITIES TO PROMOTE RESEARCH AND RECALL OF FACTS

Ask the children to:

• write a list of all the facts they know about Australia. Visit these lists later to check accuracy.

• investigate living in the interior of Australia – how to cope with the heat, water conservation, growing tourism and distances to travel.

ACTIVITIES TO PROMOTE UNDERSTANDING

Ask the children to:

• describe climate changes between the coastal areas in the north, east, south and west.

• describe how life differs living on a sheep station in the outback from living in a coastal city.

ACTIVITIES TO PROMOTE THE USE OF KNOWLEDGE AND SKILLS TO SOLVE PROBLEMS

Ask the children to:

• decide how to cross a river containing salt-water crocodiles safely.

draw a sequence of pictures to illustrate and explain the formation of coral.

ACTIVITIES TO ENCOURAGE ANALYTICAL THINKING

Ask the children to:

• discuss the best way to travel across the country, to the interior or within a city.

• write a poem describing the size of Australia, trying to give the feeling of space in the inlands and bustle of the cities.

ACTIVITIES TO PROMOTE CREATIVITY

Ask the children to:

• use collage or weaving to depict the colours of the areas of Australia – the coastal regions, the rainforest and the arid interior.

• compose a mimed Aboriginal dream sequence.

ACTIVITIES TO HELP CHILDREN USE EVIDENCE TO FORM OPINIONS AND EVALUATE CONSEQUENCES OF DECISIONS

Ask the children to:

• discuss what value and what concerns tourism brings to the Great Barrier Reef or Uluru.

• discuss the rights and traditions of the Aborigines.

B: ACTIVITIES BASED ON DIFFERENT LEARNING STYLES

ACTIVITIES FOR LINGUISTIC LEARNERS

Ask the children to:

• write a list of instructions for someone wanting to backpack across Australia.

• write a poem to illustrate the size and complexity of the country.

ACTIVITIES FOR LOGICAL AND MATHEMATICAL LEARNERS

Ask the children to:

• examine the time differences between Australia and other countries.

• identify a region and list the main features.

ACTIVITIES FOR VISUAL LEARNERS

Ask the children to:

• locate stated cities or features on a map of Australia.

• design a poster or leaflet to encourage visitors either to the country or to a particular region.

• design a menu for a barbeque.

ACTIVITIES FOR KINAESTHETIC LEARNERS

Ask the children to:

• use materials to create a representation of a famous landmark in Australia.

ACTIVITIES FOR MUSICAL LEARNERS

Ask the children to:

• compose a song, tune or rap to celebrate the coming of rain in one of the dry areas.

• learn to sing an Australian folk song.

ACTIVITIES FOR INTER-PERSONAL LEARNERS

Ask the children to:

• work in a group to develop a presentation on one aspect of Australian life.

• work as a group to develop a sketch or short play about settling in Australia as pioneers.

ACTIVITIES FOR INTRA-PERSONAL LEARNERS

Ask the children to:

• describe how they would feel if they were lost in the outback.

• look at photographs of different regions and describe the environment.

ACTIVITIES FOR NATURALISTIC LEARNERS

Ask the children to:

• prepare an argument, either for increasing tourism or limiting tourism.

LINKS ACROSS THE CURRICULUM

The *Travel Through* series of books offers up-to-date information and cross-curricular opportunities for teaching geography, literacy, numeracy, history, RE, PSHE and citizenship. The series enables children to develop an overview ('the big picture') of each country. This overview reflects the huge diversity and richness of the life and culture of each country. The series aims to prevent the development of misconceptions, stereotypes and prejudices, which often develop when the focus of a study narrows too quickly onto a small locality within a country. The books in the series help children not only to gain access to this overview, but to develop an understanding of the interconnectedness of places. They contribute to the children's geographical knowledge, skills and understanding, and help them make sense of the world around them.

Read with Mummy

My Favourite Fairytales

Story retold by Janet Brown
Illustrations by Ken Morton

ARMADILLO

3

First published in 1999 by
Armadillo Books
An imprint of Bookmart Limited
Desford Road, Enderby
Leicester LE9 5AD
England

© 1999 Bookmart Limited

Reprinted 1999

ISBN 1-90046-603-1

Printed in Singapore

My Favourite Fairytales

Contents

Goldilocks and the Three Bears

Three bears live in a house in the middle of the forest. There is a big Daddy Bear, a medium-sized Mummy Bear, and a tiny little Baby Bear.

The three bears eat porridge for breakfast. Most people like their porridge hot. But bears love cold porridge.

Mummy Bear sets the table. Then the family goes for a walk while the porridge cools down.

What do the three bears do while their porridge cools down?

9

Goldilocks is also walking in the forest. She collects berries and sings to herself. She gathers flowers.

Walking makes her hungry. The warm sun makes her sleepy. She spies a pretty house in the middle of the trees.

"Perhaps I can rest there," she thinks. "Maybe they will feed me."

She does not know that this house belongs to the three bears!

Who does the pretty house in the middle of the trees belong to?

11

Inside, the table is set for three. There are three chairs — one big chair, one medium-sized chair, and one tiny little chair.

On the table there are three bowls of porridge — one big bowl, one medium-sized bowl, and one tiny little bowl.

There are also three spoons, a jug of milk and a jar of honey.

How many places have been set at the table?

Goldilocks climbs into the big chair first. "This chair is too hard!" she says.

She tastes the porridge in the big bowl. "And this porridge is too hot!"

Next she tries the medium-sized chair. "This chair is too soft!" she says.

She tastes the porridge in the medium-sized bowl. "And this porridge is too cold!"

What is wrong with the big chair that Goldilocks climbs into first?

Goldilocks sits down in the tiny little chair. It is very comfortable. She tastes the porridge in the tiny little bowl. It is not too hot and it is not too cold.

"This is just perfect!" says Goldilocks. She eats up every last spoonful of porridge.

But Goldilocks is bigger than Baby Bear. After a while the tiny little chair starts to crack and then it breaks into pieces!

Why does Baby Bear's chair break when Goldilocks sits in it?

17

Goldilocks is tired. She goes upstairs. She finds three beds — a big bed, a medium-sized bed, and a tiny little bed.

She climbs into the big bed. "This bed is too hard!" she says.

She climbs into the medium-sized bed. "This bed is too soft!" she says.

She climbs into the tiny little bed. It is not too hard and it is not too soft.

"This is just perfect!" says Goldilocks. She falls fast asleep.

Whose bed does Goldilocks fall asleep in?

19

The bears return from the forest. "What a lovely walk!" says Daddy Bear. "Let's eat!"

Then he looks at the breakfast table.

"Somebody's been sitting on my chair!" growls Daddy Bear.

"Somebody's been sitting on my chair!" frowns Mummy Bear.

"Somebody's been sitting on my chair!" wails Baby Bear. "And they've smashed it all to pieces!"

Why do you think Baby Bear looks so sad in this picture?

They look at the bowls on the table.

"Somebody's been eating my porridge!" growls Daddy Bear.

"Somebody's been eating my porridge!" frowns Mummy Bear.

"Somebody's been eating my porridge!" wails Baby Bear. "And they've eaten it all up!"

Whose bowl is empty?

23

The three bears rush upstairs.
"Somebody's been sleeping in my bed!" roars Daddy Bear. "Somebody's been sleeping in my bed!" cries Mummy Bear. "Somebody's been sleeping in my bed!" yells Baby Bear. "AND SHE'S STILL HERE!"

At that, Goldilocks opens her eyes. She sees three hairy faces looking down at her — a big face, a medium-sized face, and a tiny little face.
"Help!" she cries. She jumps out of bed and runs all the way home.

The bears are surprised. "Was I too loud?" asks Daddy Bear. "Was I too fierce?" asks Baby Bear? "I'll make some more porridge," says Mummy Bear. "It's way past breakfast time."

Why does Baby Bear think Goldilocks is running away?

There are eight things wrong with the picture below. Can you find them?

26

On a piece of paper, practise writing these words.
Can you find them again in the story?

"This bed is too hard"

jar of honey

bowl of porridge

tiny little chair

jug of milk

Three Little Pigs

Three little pigs are looking for adventure.

They wave goodbye to their friends and go out into the big, wide world.

What do the three little pigs hope to find in the big, wide world?

The first little pig meets a man carrying straw.

"May I have some straw to build a beautiful house?" he asks.

"Certainly, little pig," says the man.

The first little pig builds himself a straw house. Then he sits down for a nap.

What does the first little pig want to do with the straw?

Nearby lives a mean and hungry wolf. The wolf knocks on the door of the straw house.

"Little pig, little pig, let me come in!" he calls.

"Not by the hair of my chinny chin chin, will I open the door and let YOU come in!" cries the little pig.

"Then I'll huff and I'll puff and I'll blow your house down!" roars the wolf.

So he huffs and he puffs and the straw house falls down. The wolf runs inside and gobbles up the first little pig.

How does the wolf make the straw house fall down?

The second little pig meets a man carrying wood.

"May I have some wood to build a large house?" he asks.

"Certainly, little pig," says the man.

The second little pig builds himself a wooden house. Then he sits down for a nap.

What does the second little pig do after he has built his house?

Soon the wolf comes knocking on the door.

"Little pig, little pig, let me come in!" he calls.

"Not by the hair of my chinny chin chin, will I open the door and let YOU come in!" cries the little pig.

"Then I'll huff and I'll puff and I'll blow your house down!" roars the wolf.

So he huffs and he puffs and he HUFFS and he PUFFS and the wooden house falls down. The wolf runs inside and gobbles up the second little pig.

What does the wolf do when he has blown down the wooden house?

The third little pig meets a man carrying bricks.

"Please may I have some bricks to build a strong house?" he asks.

"Certainly, little pig," says the man.

The third little pig builds himself a brick house. He works late into the night.

What kind of house does the third little pig want to build?

Soon the wolf comes knocking on the door.

"Little pig, little pig, let me come in!" he calls.

"Not by the hair of my chinny chin chin, will I open the door and let YOU come in!" cries the little pig.

"Then I'll huff and I'll puff and I'll blow your house down!" roars the wolf.

So he huffs and he puffs and he HUFFS and he PUFFS. Then he huffs and he puffs some more. But the brick house does not fall down!

Why do you think the third little pig's house doesn't fall down?

The next day the wolf returns.

"Little pig!" he says. "Let us go and dig turnips together tomorrow morning!"

The little pig goes to dig turnips that evening. When the wolf arrives in the morning, the field is empty and the little pig is at home eating turnip stew.

The wolf is very cross. But he says, "Little pig, let us go and pick apples together tomorrow morning!"

When the wolf arrives in the morning, the little pig is already up in the tree. "Here!" yells the little pig, and throws a juicy apple at the wolf. Then he jumps down, leaps into a barrel and rolls away down the hill to his brick house.

What does the third little pig throw at the wolf?

The wolf races after the little pig. He leaps up onto the roof of the brick house.

"I'll get you!" he roars, and climbs down the chimney.

But the little pig puts a pan of water onto the fire.
The wolf falls down the chimney and into the pan.
The little pig slams the lid on the wolf's head!
Nobody ever sees the wolf again.

And the third little pig lives happily ever after in his brick house.

What happens to the wolf when he comes down the chimney?

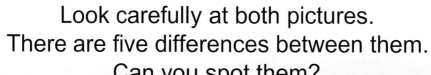

Look carefully at both pictures.
There are five differences between them.
Can you spot them?

On a piece of paper, practise writing these words.
Can you find them again in the story?

bricks

wolf

pan of water

wood

first little pig

49

Snow White and the Seven Dwarfs

Snow is falling and a black raven flies to the palace window. Inside, the Queen sits sewing. She looks up and the needle pricks her finger.

The Queen thinks, "I wish I could have a little girl with skin as white as the snow, hair as black as the raven, and lips as red as my blood."

Not long afterwards, a princess is born. She has snow-white skin, raven-black hair and blood-red lips. The King and Queen call her Snow White.

What kind of bird flies to the Queen's window?

Snow White is a beautiful and happy child. But sadly the Queen dies. The King marries again. Snow White's stepmother is beautiful but she is vain and cruel. She asks her magic mirror:

"Mirror, mirror on the wall,
Who is the fairest of them all?"

The mirror always replies:

"You, oh Queen, are the fairest of them all."

Who tells the new Queen that she is fairest of them all?

But every year Snow White is growing more beautiful. One day the mirror tells the Queen:

"You, oh Queen, are fair, it's true,
But Snow White is more fair than you!"

The Queen is furious. She orders a hunter to take Snow White into the forest and kill her.

But Snow White is kind and pure. The hunter loves her too much to kill her. He tells her to run away. Then he tells the Queen that Snow White is dead.

Why doesn't the hunter kill Snow White?

Snow White is tired and hungry. She is scared and lonely. She wanders into the forest until she sees a house.

Inside, the table is set for dinner. There are seven little chairs and seven little bowls. Snow White takes a little food from each bowl.

Upstairs there are seven little beds. Snow White climbs into one of the beds. She falls fast asleep.

How many people do you think live in the house in the forest?

The house belongs to seven dwarfs. All day long they dig for diamonds on the mountain.

In the evening when they return home, they see that somebody has taken food from each bowl. They go upstairs and there in one of the seven little beds is Snow White!

Snow White tells the seven dwarfs about the wicked Queen. They invite her to stay with them. They build her a chair and a bed.

What do the seven dwarfs do on the mountain all day long?

The wicked Queen thinks Snow White is dead. She is as vain as ever. She asks her mirror:

"Mirror, mirror on the wall
Who is the fairest of them all? "

But the mirror replies:

"You, oh Queen, are fair, it's true,
But Snow White is more fair than you!"

The Queen is furious. She decides to kill Snow White herself!

Who does the mirror think is the fairest of them all now?

The Queen dresses as a beggar. When the seven dwarfs have gone to work, the beggar knocks on the door.

"You are such a pretty young thing!" says the beggar to Snow White. "Will you take an apple from a poor, old woman?"

Snow White bites into the rosy, red apple. But the apple is poisoned! Snow White falls down dead. The beggar throws off her disguise.

"Now I am the fairest of them all!" cries the wicked Queen.

Who is the beggar really?

The seven dwarfs weep and wail. They build Snow White a glass coffin, and take her to the top of a hill. They guard her night and day.

One day a prince rides by. He sees Snow White lying there. Her skin is white as snow, her hair is black as a raven, and her lips are red as blood.

"How beautiful she is!" says the prince. He lifts her head to kiss her. The piece of poisoned apple flies out of Snow White's mouth.

Snow White opens her eyes – she is alive! The seven dwarfs dance for joy.

What happens when the prince kisses Snow White?

In the palace, the mirror tells the wicked Queen:

*"You, oh Queen, are fair, it's true
But Snow White is STILL more fair than you!"*

The Queen flies into a rage and is never heard of again.

Snow White marries the handsome prince and they live happily ever after!

Who gets married and lives happily ever after?

On a piece of paper, practise writing these words:

sweeping up

basket

pick axe

beggar

shovel

Look carefully at the seven dwarfs below.

Find three dwarfs with caps pointing to the left.

Which three dwarfs have just one tooth?

71

The Ugly Duckling

Mother Duck is very excited. Her eggs are nearly ready to hatch. Soon she will be the proud mother of six little ducklings.

Her friend says, "One of your eggs is much bigger than the others."

"ALL my little ducklings will be beautiful," sniffs Mother Duck.

Secretly she is worried. But she does not want the other farmyard animals to know that.

How many little ducklings are about to be born?

75

It's time! Five eggs start to crack, and five fluffy ducklings wriggle out of their shells.

"Ahhh!" say all the farmyard animals.

Then the sixth egg, the BIG egg, starts to crack. And out steps a very strange bird.

"Oh!" cry the farmyard animals. Then they look at Mother Duck. She pretends not to notice that her sixth baby is a very ugly duckling indeed.

What does Mother Duck pretend not to notice about her sixth duckling?

Mother Duck and her six ducklings go for a swim.
Five little ducklings splish splash together in the
water. But the sixth duckling is too big to play with
the others.

"Ouch!" they cry. "Go away, Ugly Duckling!" They
swim away from him, laughing. The Ugly Duckling is
unhappy. He decides to run away. But wherever he
goes, things are always the same.

"What an ugly duckling!" cry the wild ducks.
"What a strange bird!" cry the geese.
"Go away!" they cry.
"One day," thinks the Ugly Duckling, "I will be
beautiful, and then they'll be sorry." But he does not
believe it.

What do the Ugly Duckling's brothers and sisters say to him?

The Ugly Duckling is strong and brave. But he is also lonely, and winter is coming. He makes himself a home by the side of a big lake. One morning he wakes up and watches a family of swans flying across the sky.

"How graceful they are!" he thinks. "How happy they must be!"

He sighs. It is getting colder.

Where does the Ugly Duckling make his new home?

Snow begins to fall. The lake freezes over. In the distance the Ugly Duckling can see a farmhouse. There are bright lights and voices.

"I wish I lived over there," he thinks to himself.

But he knows they will only laugh at him.

So he goes out onto the frozen lake instead. His big feet make wonderful skates. The Ugly Duckling skates on the ice for hours. He has fun by himself.

What does the Ugly Duckling do out on the lake by himself?

The ice melts. Spring has come! The other birds start to arrive back at the lake. The water is full of wild ducks and geese, chattering and laughing. They are glad to be together again.

The Ugly Duckling hides. He waits for someone to notice him, but everyone is busy.

Why have the other birds started to arrive back at the lake?

"I don't care," says the Ugly Duckling. He notices everyone else flying around. He stretches his wings and begins to flap. Suddenly he is up in the sky, away from the chattering voices.

"I can fly!" he cries.

The sky is very blue. Up here it is quiet. He feels the sun on his wings. The wind slips past him. It feels wonderful.

Do you recognise the Ugly Duckling in this picture?
Can you guess what has happened? 87

He flies past a family of swans.

"My goodness!" they say. "What a handsome bird!"

The Ugly Duckling turns around in surprise. "ME?" he asks.

"A most fine and handsome bird!" say the swans. "One of the most beautiful we have ever seen!"

The Ugly Duckling is so surprised that he crashes down into the lake. The he looks into the water to see his reflection.

A snowy white swan is looking back up at him!

What does the Ugly Duckling see reflected in the lake?

All the swans crowd around him. "He must be a prince," they say. "We would like to be his friend."

"Where do you come from?" they ask. "Why haven't we seen you before?"

The Beautiful Swan smiles. "I've been here all the time!" he says.

What is the Ugly Duckling's new name?

On a piece of paper, practise writing these words:

flying south

nest

eggs

swan

duckling

Trace with your finger along the path and help the
Ugly Duckling find his way to the pond.